Sifting Through the Ashes of Me

The Early Poems

Jay Walker

Sifting Through the Ashes of Me: The Early Poems. Copyright © 2019 Jay Walker. Produced and printed by Stillwater River Publications. All rights reserved. Written and produced in the United States of America. This book may not be reproduced or sold in any form without the expressed, written permission of the author and publisher.

Visit our website at www.StillwaterPress.com for more information.

First Stillwater River Publications Edition

ISBN-13: 978-1-946-30096-6
ISBN-10: 1-946-30096-9

1 2 3 4 5 6 7 8 9

Written by Jay Walker
Published by Stillwater River Publications, Pawtucket, RI, USA.

The views and opinions expressed in this book are solely those of the author and do not necessarily reflect the views and opinions of the publisher.

The First Edition Was Dedicated to My Child…
This Edition Is Dedicated to My Mom, Dolly.

Table of Contents

Inspired through Lack of Inspiration 9
Wake Up! 11
To Luke in Utero 14
Dreaming... 17
What Colors 19
Time to Do 22
God 25
A Midsummer's Day in New England 27
Repentance 30
No Such Thing (A Play on Words) 31
Pencil 33
The "Not Another Revolution" Poem 35
You Said 38
My Eyes 39
Contact 42
The Circle 44
The Rain 48
Red, White & Blue 50
No Master of Time 52
Her Level 56
Freaky 58
Katchupa [for Quintin & Renegade] 61
Decent Exposure 62
Watch/er 65
Here 68
Slammed 70
Message for the Millennium 72
Tainted 75
Weight 77
Male Nursing 81
It All Started When... [A Writing Exercise] 83
Haiku Hell 87
Days Go By 89
Brother 91
Jay Walker Day 93

True Colors 94
What I Want 97
Contemplation 98
Sometimes… 102
Now How Much Would You Pay? 103
Random Haiku, Senryu & Tanka 108
Paying for Past Crimes 111
Anakin's Lament 114
Magnetic 117
Remembering to Breathe 119
March 20th, 2003 123
Numb to the Gift 126
Your Fox to Her Grapes 128
Jukebox 130
Sifting Through the Ashes of Me 138

Inspired through Lack of Inspiration

I want to scream poetry at the top of my lungs
    but I've no fire in my breath
I want to cry waterfalls
    fluid flowing forming phrases on pages
        but my wells are tear-dry
I want to use my pen as a razorblade
    Slash! My! Everywhere!
        and ooze my blackness onto this paper
            but my blood is not black
        it is red burning flame alive
            pumping passion for life through my heart
I want to write a powerful
    heart-ripping
    gut-wrenching
    soul-shattering
    magnificent piece of work
  but my best poetry comes out of darkness
    and my world is full of light
        like at the end of a long, dark tunnel
            illuminating all around
            illuminating me
                lifting me up
                    floating
                        in heavenly
                            light
                    I feel no pain …

Life's so good, I can't write poetry, dammit!

That makes me mad

    makes me frustrated

    makes me want to scream poetry at the top of my …

                                          wait a minute

Wake Up!

Hey.

Hey, wake up.

Did you hear that?

That noise –

There it is again!

It sounded like a door closing

A door closing down the hall

    as a burglar steals the fine china to feed his stomach

        or his habit.

Mother!

Mother, wake up!

Did you hear that sound?

It sounded like a baby crying

    crying so loud and long until it's hoarse

        just so that someone, anyone will hear,

            but its cries go unnoticed

                or ignored.

Father, wake up!

I hear the door close on a confessional

    as a father goes to commit sins of his own,

I hear the door close on a police car

    as a man of justice joins in an injustice of his own,

And I hear windows smashing

    as the people demand that justice be served.

I hear the cell door close on a man accused of a crime

    due to the color of his skin,

        not the blood which may or may not be on his hands,

And I hear hammers pounding two boards of wood together
>   just so someone can burn them.

Can't you hear it?

Wake up, my sister!
Can't you hear the sounds of people shouting back and forth –
>   religion vs. rights – to the point of riot,

While the door to the clinic closes
>   On a life that didn't have the chance to begin,

Or the door to some power-hungry bureaucrat's office closes
>   as he sits behind his desk, making laws
>> telling you what you can and cannot do with your bodies,
>>> as if he's God,

Or the parents' door closes in the face
>   of a child with child
>> as they close the subject of it being even an issue,
>>> let alone a possibility.

Can't you hear the sound of a man's fist slamming into a woman's face,
>   just because she asked him where he was going,
>> or because he had a hard day at work,
>>> or whatever reason he thought of?

Wake up, my brother!
Listen to the guns firing overseas,
>   as men fight for what they don't understand
>> and rich men protect their money.

Listen to the guns firing just down the block,
>   as a boy who barely finished high school is killed
>> because he wears the wrong color
>>> or *is* the wrong color.

Listen to the sounds of cars crashing into poles or each other
>because the driver didn't know when to stop
>>at the bar down the road.

Listen to the door close on a bedroom,
>where the mind of an ignorant
>>*macho*
>>>sexist man closes on even the thought
>that no means *no*.

Wake up!
Hear the door close on a factory
>closed down, putting people out of work,
>>because no one trusted their own country.

Hear the door close on a courtroom –
>one of many –
>>that's forgotten just who the victim is.

Hear the door close on a car
>that someone, for the past year,
>>has called home.

Can't you hear it?
It's not just overseas or in the ghettos or in back alleys of big cities.
Listen!
Listen to the door close and the window smash
>on a car in a gas station right across the street!

Listen!
Can't you hear it?
Are you listening?
Hey,
>wake up.

To Luke in Utero

I lay my hands upon your walls & feel my whole world turning
You pace your space as much as your ol' man, but
    you spend your whole time awake
        just waiting for sleep to come
Everything you need is handed to you
    all pre-processed & digested
        yet I can still hear your heart beating 150 times a minute
What could possibly make you so anxious in there?
Do you know what awaits you on the outside?
Do you feel the cold cruelty of the bad air of humanity
    against your delicate skin?
Does the thought make you cry out even before your first breath?
Do you fear the voice calling to you each night
    whispering low
        "Luke, I am your father."
Do you envision a dark & evil figure looming over you
    manipulating your destiny to his will?
Will those whispered words be what really illicit your first tears?
Could your high-decibel, monosyllabic vocabulary
    really just be a strained attempt at questioning?
Is "Waaaah"
    a "Whyyyy" we just don't understand?
    "Whyyyy did you deliver me into this damaged & doomed world?
    Whyyyy couldn't I just stay in my womb?
    Whyyyy couldn't you corral the stallion just long enough
        for the world to find peace
           or fall to pieces?
    What were you thinking?"

I wasn't.

To be honest, my mind wasn't working at the time

Scientifically, I could say that the oxygenated blood had been
    occupying a different organ
        but I don't believe in science, anymore

Statistically, I could say that Ortho Tri Cyclen is over 99% effective
    & we just did it more than 100 times
        but never tell me the odds
    because I believe in fate
        believe in destiny
        believe you had sentience as sperm
            swam your way through walls of protection
            brought fertilization to my salvation

Yes, I needed saving from myself
        from my self-destructive plans for a future
    that really had no future

With the bellowing bugle of the blue strip that heralded your coming
    I was forced to snap to attention
        gain focus
      & a mature adult materialized
        where once there was none

I believe you are my savior
    you are magic
    you are meant to be

The Force is strong with you, my son

So, while you may now look at me with disdain
    wondering why I brought you into this world
        or brought this world to you
    I answer that I had no control

I cannot mold the universe to my will

I am not Lord over the Sith
    or anyone else, for that matter
I'm just barely getting used to being master of my *own* fate
    but for you, I will learn
I will learn to feel the Force flow through me
    learn all the gifts God has wrapped for me
        hidden like Easter eggs in the Garden of this galaxy
    learn to unwrap the gift of myself for all the world
    as it is reborn every minute
I will do, for "do not" is no longer a choice
    & Yoda said, "There is no try."
I cannot make this a world worthy of you
    but I can make myself the father you need me to be
        no dark figure looming in the background
        just a man
            and yet
        not just any man
        the only man who can be me
            who will love you
        with all a father can give
            who will be by your side
                be your teacher *and* student
        & we will rule our galaxy as father & son
    & the Force will be with you
            always.

Dreaming...

I wish you woke me up before you started having sex with me.
I was still asleep
Asleep
       and dreaming …
Dreaming of you and me.
Dreaming of the feelings I thought we shared.
Dreaming of the life that we could've had together.
Dreaming I was making love to you.
But I never dreamed …

I never dreamed it would never last
  never dreamed that we weren't meant to be
  never dreamed those feelings –
      feelings that were stronger than I've ever felt –
         were nothing more than animal attraction
      feelings of passion were no more than lust
        and the longing I felt for you
          the need to be near you
            to be with you
              always
            was purely physical.
I never dreamed it was only sex.
I never dreamed …

When we first met, we both fell into the dream,
    caught up in this feeling of fire
            of euphoria
            of passionate, ignorant bliss,
But you woke up before me
    and fulfilled your lust
        while you let me dream.
I wish you woke me up before you started having sex with me.
I know we'd have had to wake up eventually.
It's just that, even now,
    I'm still half-asleep.

What Colors

This is a tale of two colors

He

    was dark

Not "dark & mysterious" dark

        more like "burnt" dark

                burnt by society

                burnt by centuries of oppression

                slow burning in his soul

                like a slow roast coffee dark

                        dark & bitter

                                  until there was her

She

    was light

Brighter than a thousand of the sons that seared his skin

        lighting his dark coffee existence

            like her smooth cream skin was liquid

                pouring into his cup of life

They made life more flavorful

        blending together for a sweet, rich

                            gray?

Wait a minute ...

If coffee is black & cream is white

        wouldn't that make your drink gray?

What is the color of the world

        as it spins by the eye in this black universe?

Do not take only the ocean blue

        reflected in the mirror sky

Do not consider solely the still snowcaps of mountains

        or the similarly white of passing clouds

Take into account, but not by itself
    the rolling green hills or rainbow of hues in the flower garden
For that would be as some look at skin
    and see only black & white
        red & yellow
        half & half
        mixed
    and think this is how to live life
But life is always moving
      moving faster than tsunami
      blowing by faster than a hurricane
It is the flash of lightning
    but still faster
Life taught electric skies how to burn
    and our fire is still burning
    the world keeps on turning
        billions upon billions of miles per hour
        keeps on turning
      faster than eagle eye can see
        keeps on turning
          twirling to a blur
            blending all the colors of the world
            to brown
So he is not black
    but a deep, rich, soulful brown
She is not white
    but a light, soft, creamy brown
And we are not separated like crayons in a box

We are all just shades and hues of brown
        beautifully blending & blurring into the blessed
                brown
The color of all the world is brown
There.
Now that *that's* settled
        I think it's time we moved on.

Time to Do

Who said that every wish would be heard and answered
    when wished on the morning star?
Somebody thought of that and someone …
    was full of crap!
There's never been any descending debris
No meteorite held any magic or mysticism for me
    [It's 11:09]
You ask me why my head hangs low
    why I look to the ground
I tell you looking skyward betrays me
    shining stars deceive
And when the brightness of truth is false,
    all that's left is darkness
    [It's 11:10]
And tossin' coins in a fountain
    Ain't nothin' but watchin' money drown
You say, "Better than hopes and dreams,"
    but I say my change is better spent on the tax for my tea
        than to sacrifice its life for the resurrection of something
        as useless as a wish
May as well cut out the middle man
    hand it right to the homeless
    save them the worry of getting wet
I don't mean to bring you down
    but better to dampen spirits than clothing, right?
    [It's 11:11]

It's 11:11!

Will you make a wish?

Will you waste breath better spent just breathing?

It's 11:11!

Will you waste brain power trying to think

    of who's thinking of you at 11:11?

Is it the same person you're thinking of?

Are they the same thoughts?

And what do you think

    what do you do

        what have you done to make thoughts reality

            to turn fantasy from fiction to fact

Face facts!

Nothing comes to dreamers but dreams, ooh, I said,

    sitting idle in a boat, while everyone else is down the stream.

And nothing comes from an eyelash but dead hair fallen

Wishes from fallen follicles is a falsehood

        a façade

        a fucking lie!

But I know you can't just will wishes into reality

I know I have the power to control my destiny

Now, don't misunderstand me

    don't mistake my message for one of misery, y'see

I have a dream, like the good Dr. did

        like all the doctors did

            but the doctors knew

And the lawyers and the teachers

    the hitters and the hoopsters

        they knew, too

Cowboys and carnival clowns, actors and astronauts, they all knew
Dreams don't make themselves come true!
Do.

Look, an eyelash.
What did you wish for?

God

It is truth revealed

It is the light that shines

It is the one true way

    and all ways

It is everything we know and believe

    and more than we could possibly imagine

It is the Lord and the Lady

    man and woman

    both and neither

It is as new as a child from the womb

    and older than the sands of time

It is Yahweh, Jesus, Allah and Goddess

It is science

    and it is magick

It is the energy and essence of the earth itself

It *is* the earth and the sun and the moon

It is the universe

It is everything and everyone and everywhere

I see it

I see it in the hustle and bustle of city life

    and in the peaceful countryside

I see it in every sunrise

    and in every sunset

    and in the sacred moon

I see it in the eyes of a child

    wide-eyed and innocent, eager to experience life

I see it in the eyes of the old

    wise in the ways of the world

I see it in the magic of the new technology
      erasing the borders of the world
           opening it up
                and making it smaller
I see it in the true magick of the old ways
      making use of the wonders this world offers
           or in the wonder for just taking in the world around you
                or in reading a book and opening new worlds
                    with your imagination
And I see it in all the faces around me
I hear it in all the words spoken tonight
I see it
  feel it all around me
      inside me
It surrounds me
  flows through me
      with me
  becomes part of me
It *is* me
It is *you* … and you … and you
It is all of us
It is everyone and everything and everywhere
Reach out!
Reach out with your hands and hearts and souls and touch it
                                feel it
Feel it with everything you are
           were
           and aspire to be

Open your eyes and see it everywhere

Close your eyes and see it like you've never seen it before

Listen

Hear it in the words I'm speaking

Hear it in your own words in your head

Hear it in the city

Hear it in the earth

Hear it all around you

Hear it

See it

Feel it

It is life.

A Midsummer's Day in New England

I sit on my porch on a midsummer's day.
The sun shines brightly on my face;
The air is warm and comfortable;
A cool breeze blows through the trees
      In the fields and the parks and the yards.
A beautiful midsummer's day.

I sit on my porch on a midsummer's day.
I sit by myself, as I think of my life,
My ups, my downs, my good times and bad;
I sit and I think of the times that I've spent
      On this earth, in my home, in my life.
The breeze blows slightly stronger.

I sit on my porch on a midsummer's day.
My childhood days are still on my mind,
Like old photographs in a family album
Or videotapes played over and over:
      Play, pause, fast forward, rewind.
Marshmallow clouds fill the sky.

I sit on my porch on a midsummer's day.
My thoughts are still turned toward my life,
All my friends, my family, my foes,
The people and places and things in my life,
      My dislikes, my laughs, my loves.
           The clouds grow more and darker.

I sit on my porch on a midsummer's day.

I think that the bad times outweigh the good,

 My life filled with sadness and heartache and pain,

The times when I felt so cold inside;

My heart grows sad and lonely.

The clouds, they fill the sky.

I sit on my porch on a midsummer's day.

I think of the one who has captured my heart,

The woman whom I can never have,

My love who, yet, will never be mine

To have, to hold, to love.

Do you see the lightning?

I sit on my porch on a midsummer's day.

I cannot stop thinking of these things that sadden;

As hard as I try, I cannot stop feeling

That coldness, that chill that you feel when you think

    How you've spent your life alone.

Can you feel the thunder?

I sit on my porch on a midsummer's day.

I do not feel as I had felt before;

I do not feel joyous; my soul now feels empty;

I cannot stop my soul's crying out

    As tears roll down my face.

Rain begins to fall.

I sit on my porch on a midsummer's day.

as the rain falls softly

down.

Repentance

Winter without snow
Brings summer far too rainy
Ceaseless showers slay

I danced in the rain
That washed people's lives away
My penance, these haiku

Cry, relentless sky!
Shed the tears for those you killed
With the tears you shed

Finally, the sun
Comes to dry the water that
Both gave and took life

Unexpected sun
Is nature's apology
For days of downpour

I enjoyed the rain
Never knowing that it killed
For that, I'm sorry

No Such Thing (A Play on Words)

Fuck.

I fuck.

I don't have sex; I don't "make love;"

I fuck.

I fuck you.

I fuck you over and over again,

As you fuck me over again,

As you fuck me over …

In my life, I've fucked – and I've been fucked.

I've fucked over and over – and I've been fucked over.

When I was younger, I thought I was "making love,"

I thought I was being made love to,

But I was fucked.

I was fucked …

Every time I thought I was in love,

Every time I thought I was loved,

I got fucked,

And fucked over …

Now I know.

There's no such thing as "making love;"

There's no such thing as love.

There's only fucking,

So now I fuck.

I don't have sex; I don't "make love;"

Now I know better.

Now I fuck.

I fuck you – over and over,

As you fuck me over …

As you fuck me …

Fuck me …

Fuck.

Pencil

You know what God's problem was?

He didn't use pencil.

God never used pencil to create anything

Think about it!

He molded man from the clay of the earth

    the same earth he raised to form mountain peaks

        lowered for great canyon depths

        burrowed for caverns and crevices

        flooded with ocean

    and left it to bake in the kiln-fire sun

        bake 'til hard

            hard-headed

            hard-hearted

        not noticing flaws until too late

Then, after

    after he creates this imperfection

        he has the Ten Commandments *carved in stone!*

How can He be so confident

    that such a flawed creature

        would find these instructions easy to follow?

Some of us can't even follow directions for making canned soup!

And the Devil's no better

Everything always has to be signed in blood

    just as he used his own blood, sweat & tears

        to permanently scribe his eternal place

            in our spiritual history

What the Hell were they thinking?
Couldn't an omniscient being
      see this shit coming?
Shouldn't the knowledge of everything that is, was & will be
      give you some sort of advantage?
And little loopy loser Lucifer
      the other side to the Almighty's coin
           and formerly his right-hand man
Wouldn't you think that an omniscient & omnipotent being
      would stop your stupid overthrow attempt before it even started
           if He thought you had any chance in Hell for success?
           (pardon the pun)
Now he enlists the sorry souls of the Maker's mistakes
      sad sacks in his Armageddon army
Does he actually think he can win next time?
Forget the Word of God
I've got a word of advice:
      take it from a poet
They call them works in progress for a reason
Sometimes things transform from feeling to the unintended
Sometimes you start with one message in mind
      and say something else you needed to say
           but not what you wanted to
      you still need to express the original thought
Sometimes the best word to use comes after the piece is written
Sometimes you wish a piece could just be forgotten
So take it from a poet & create in pencil
It makes mistakes
      easy to erase.

The "Not Another Revolution" Poem

Okay, let's get things straight right from the start
I am *not* going to do another revolution poem
I am not about jumping on the bandwagon
    to the next battlefield
        fighting alongside mere babes who
            eat their own bunk until their bellies are full &
                fling it at the walls until they're bored
I am *not* going to do another revolution poem
I do not want to be herded into this
    crowd of sheeple bleating the word like a ma-a-antra
        beating the word
            the concept into the ground &
            the world into submission
I am *not* going to do another revolution poem
I don't want to be grouped with the latest wave of revolutionaries
    who don't even know why they're fighting
        don't even know who came before them
        don't even know what poem they're sampling
I am *not* going to do another revolution poem
The revolution *has* been televised
        & commercialized
        & popularized
The revolution has been pasteurized
        homogenized
        immunized
    & otherwise sterilized

The revolution has been plagiarized
                monopolized
              & standardized
          it has been philosophized
             then bastardized
             & demonized
The revolution has been canceled due to lack of enrollment
The revolution has been
        has been
        has been!
     it ha-ppened
                where ya' been, man?
I am *not* going to do another revolution poem
      because I do not want to be part of another revolution
          do not want to be treated like an animal &
                left lurking in the window
          watching pigs cavort with humans
              not being able to tell between them
         do not want to be part of a movement
            that only serves to bring me
              right back to where I started
We evolved into systems that weren't working
     & changed them
        into systems that weren't working
          so we revolted, replacing them
        with systems that weren't working
           so we developed them
    into systems

                that weren't

                      working

Spins me so dizzy I'm sick to my stomach

             sick of democracies & aristocracies

          full of hypocrisies & fallacies

        sick of the next

                feudalismcommunismcapitalismsocialism schism

            to come around

        sick of the sickness *not* inherent in the systems

         but in the people using them

The systems are flawed because people are flawed

                    are filled with materialistic

                        self-serving ideals

    that just aren't working

We don't need another movement for revolution

We need to *move* & *be* moved

           to real *change*

That starts from within each and every one of us

    and I'm starting with me.

You Said

You said you wanted me to complete the journey to manhood
    then stood in the middle of the road
You said you wanted me to stand on my feet
    then held my hand
        held me down
You said you wanted me to act like an adult
    then scolded me like a child
You said you wanted me to fight for what was right
    as long as it wasn't you I was fighting against
You said you wanted to shelter me from the world until I was ready
    then constantly brought it into the home
You said you wanted me to take responsibility for my home
    then, in the same breath,
        you told me it wasn't mine
You said you wanted me to be my own man
    then force-fed me ethics of yours
        and of others
        'til I was sick of your home cooking
        then insisted that your medicine
            was better than mine
You said I wasn't listening to you
    and you screamed it loud enough
        so that you couldn't hear me
You said that you did it all out of love
    then, in the same breath,
        you refused to find the middle ground
            that could make us *both* happy

You said I didn't know what love was
    but I'm the one who listened
        to every word you said.

My Eyes

Tonight, I am blind
My eyes lay in the skies outside
Round clouds crowd the shroud of night
    and I am blind
I see nobody
I see no body
    no height
    no girth
    no age limit to the soul
I see no colors
    no color lines
    no border lines
    no boundaries to the heart
They say don't sweat the little things
    and everything is small
I say don't *see* the little things
    so I am blind to all
        but I can still hear you
           still hear your words
                your beautiful words
                    painting portraits in my mind
                so vivid, I don't need my eyes
I can still feel the infinite dimensions of your soul
    with the fingertips of my own
        and I don't need my eyes

My other senses are heightened infinitely
    sending swirling visions of yesterday
        and of tomorrow
        and of now
        and of now
        and of
          now
    and I don't need my eyes
        to see the infinite beauty in this room, and

Look.

Look.

The sky is crying.

Contact

I am running my hand over your curves in my mind
                                                            slowly

I am tracing my finger along every line of your body
        every place your muscles define
        every vertebra in your spine

I am allowing my palm contact
    skin on skin
        sinful pleasure of the imagination

I am placing parted lips on the curve between neck & shoulder
        between nipple & rib cage
        between rib & hip
        between buttock & thigh

I am kissing every crevice
    tongue darting in every divot & dimple
    lingering in the navel awhile

In fantasy, I am in every picture
    sliding shining skins together
        at once caressing & being caressed

In this one, you can see my arm
    stretching across smooth stomach
        hand on your hip

In this one here, my body lies next to yours
    your backside just long enough
        to conveniently conceal parts
            too ugly for what's happening here

No, this part shall not enter this fantasy
>> will not enter you here
> no matter how close it comes

This is not about sex

This is about sweet sensuality

This is about intimacy without intercourse

This is about everything that matters
> everything that is
>> everything that everything is ever about

This is about contact
> about touching you
> about becoming a part of you
>> becoming one with you
> in sinful purity & sensual innocence

This is not about penetration
> except for the glass
>> that separates our realities.

The Circle

I had the dream again last night.
I dreamed I woke up – and was trapped in a room,
Trapped in a room only big enough for one,
A room with no doors, no windows, no furniture,
No light ...
And then I woke up.
What do you think that means?

I had the dream again last night.
I dreamed I woke up and was trapped in the room,
But the room had a window where the light shone through,
But I couldn't reach it to see outside,
I couldn't ... reach ...
And then I woke up.
What do you think that means?

I had the dream again last night.
I dreamed I woke up in the room,
But this time I could reach the window,
And I looked outside toward the light ...
And I saw ...

An angel.
Her voice called out to me with a sound so shrill and yet
      so beautiful
And with her cries the walls to my room came crumbling down

And as I stood amidst the rubble,

    freed from my prison,

    staring into the heavenly eyes of my savior,

She came to me

She reached out her hand

    and touched my heart

FIRE!

Flames like I had never seen, heat like I had never felt surged through me

        set me ablaze

    and when they stopped

        I looked …

          and I had wings.

Wings so majestic and wondrous and outstretched

    reaching for the sky

    yearning to ***FLY!***

I leapt up and suddenly I was off!

        I was flying!

        I was soaring high above,

So high above the houses and the streets,

    and the trees and the mountains,

        and the clouds

So high above

    everything.

In the distance, I saw the rays of the sun over the vast ocean waters

    as it began its slow descent into slumber

And I heard the ocean call to me,

    as it so often does.

I flew to it
    and soared above it

        and glided over this waving blanket of blue silk
And I watched the giant golden orb melt into the horizon,
    sending out streaks of reds & golds & hues of indescribable beauty
I called for my angle to share this with me
She spread her wings and climbed higher
        higher into the sky
    her luminescent image sweeping across the color-streaked canvas,
        where night fought day for control
She came up behind me
    and _**ripped my wings out!**_
FALLING!
I'm falling through the air like a jet on fire,
    my mouth hung open, frozen in a silent scream,
        pain surging through my body
Falling farther, faster, closer to the waves of water which
    once looked so inviting
        but now look back at me with a fast hard coldness

I smashed into the surface like it was concrete
        and felt every bone in my body shatter into a million pieces
            along with my heart
And as I sank slowly to the ocean floor
        I reached out and called to my angel
            who could only look down at me with her sad eyes
        crying tears of gold and crimson
            flooding the ocean further above my head
                until the glittering rays of sunset
                    and the light from the twinkling stars
                of the approaching night sky
                    no longer reached my eyes
And feeling the icy fingers of Poseidon's kingdom
        envelop my body
        push the air from me
        and claim me as their own
            drowning under the weight of my own sadness
                I slowly surrender to the surrounding darkness.

And then I woke up
Trapped in a room only big enough for one,
A room with no doors, no windows, no furniture,
No light …
And then I woke up.
What do you think that means?

What do you think that means?

The Rain

Here comes the rain again
The sky is an indecisive shade today
   can't make up its mind to be blue or gray today
     used to know the feeling
   can't make up its mind to rain or shine today
     used to know the feeling,
       not knowing whether to smile or cry
But lately I realized that rain is not the sky cryin'
   but the Earth washing away the garbage
     & giving itself nourishment
So I let the rain fall down on me
   fallin' on my head like a memory,
     fallin' on my head like a new emotion
       a new feeling
    love secure
    lovin' on solid ground
    not afraid of land mines where I step anymore
It makes me wish you were here with me
I want you here now
I want to walk in the open breeze
    the gentle breeze of your loving support
   putting air in my lungs & wind in my sails
   pushing me onward

I want to kiss like lovers do
        like we did our first night together
            or when dancing in the rain
            or when I said goodbye
want to dive into your ocean of love so deep
                so pure
                so full of life & possibilities
                so seemingly endless
I used to know what it felt like to be indecisive like the sky
Now, I know what I want
        so, tell me, lover
            is it raining with you?

Red, White & Blue

The sky was blue
The sky was shimmering crystal blue
    starred & striped by the white of cumulus
The air, though
The air was red
    red with the flash & excitement of the city
    red with the ripeness of the Big Apple
        begging to be bitten
    red with the high stress on man's engine
        as capitalism pushes the pedal to the floor
    red with the building pressure
        put on humanity by the need for green
    red with the nervous anticipation of the
    red danger yet to come
Then it came
    it came shooting through the air with a rocket's red glare
Two white missiles came crashing through blue glass & steel
    & a burst of red flame turned the sky black
Then the air flashed red-white-red-white &
    red-blue-red-blue
    as red-blooded heroes in blue & white uniforms
        rushed to answer thousands of cries for help
The air was red with screaming
    & we were white with shock at what happened
        not knowing that worse was in store

Then it happened

The sky shook with blue thunder

    as white-knuckled masses yearned to be free

        from the frightening freefall

One hundred ten stories later

    five thousand stories end

        & thousands more begin

They begin with the red of blood that stains the streets

    with the white dust settling on buildings

        suddenly tall again

    with the salty blue ocean of tears

        washing on this country's shores

            from the opposite direction

    & black clouds shroud a mourning country

        where its symbols of prosperity & achievement once stood

Then red blood flows through tubes

    as people give so others can simply live

Then angels spread white wings

    stitching lives together with hope

Then boys in blue bring brothers from the wreckage

    – & we are *all* brothers now –

        & I see the sliver of white hope

            in the eyes of Lady Liberty

                until …

The blue eyes of Uncle Sam turn red with rage

The flag wavers wave feverishly red

The air is red with the screams of revenge

Soon the white shrouds of Islam
        blackened by the stigma of extremists
                become red from the hatred of small minds
                      despite allegiance to *our* flag
Soon white ships cross blue oceans
        so that black jets can rain red on distant shores
                & while most give patriotic cheers
    some of us still sing the blues
            still cry those blue, salty tears
        seeking to flood the world with red love
                make it an ark from which to rebuild itself
                send the white dove of peace
                      to carry back an olive branch in its beak
                marvel at the rainbow colors of humanity
While most wave the flag blindly
        some of us can see the colors & what they truly stand for:
            the red of love
            the white of peace
            & the clear blue of the sky
                where our eagles fly free …
                where we *all* fly free.

No Master of Time

If I could turn back time
If I could find a way
I'd take back those words
    take back those words
    take back those words
               you never heard me say
take back those feelings that never really saw the light of day
take back the brain power wasted on fantasies
    I knew would never come to pass
take back all the time wasted on a friendship
    I never could've guessed wouldn't last
If I could turn back time
If I could find a way
I never would've opened my heart to you about all those women
    knowing you'd forget it all
        just when I needed someone to remember
I never would've let you open your heart to me
    knowing it was more poisoned than mine
I never would've opened my home to you
    knowing you'd rob me blind
        of more than just money
I never would've let you open your home to me
    knowing the hospitality was all show

If I could turn back time
I would've avoided the café where you worked
        the neighborhood where you lived
        the late-night restaurant where we met
If I could, I'd go back to make sure I never met you
        make sure your parents never met each other
        make sure your ancestors never met evolution
If I could, I'd rewrite the alphabet
        & put U & I as far away as possible
    rewrite the Bible
        & give Lilith *your* name
    rewrite the universe
        & let there be light *without* your brand of darkness
But I am no master of time
I can only learn to master myself
    the way I couldn't then
I can only learn to master my pain
    not scream at the knife in my back
        like I did when you put it there
I can only learn to master my heart
    not open it so easily
    not give pieces to strangers
        like candy to children who ring your door for treats
            but play nasty tricks anyway

I can only master my path
      walk the high road from here
           instead of sinking to your level
                as I had before

If I could turn back time
If I could find a way
I'd take back those words that hurt you
    & you'd go, anyway

But I am no master of time
I can only learn to master myself
      so I extend this open hand to you
           but only to keep you at a distance.

Her Level

You said you admire her intelligence
        her degree
        her knowledge of the classics
            of mythology
She told you she needed someone on her level
She left you rubbing your red face
        stinging with the imprint of her hand
            while she was oblivious to the fact
                that she even slapped you
            but you were *both* deaf to the bigger blow she delivered
                to herself
Had she bothered to look into your eyes
        she would've seen the fires of Troy burning inside you
            would've seen the green eyes of Othello &
                Birnamwood come to Dunsinane
Had she bothered to look at your back when placing the knife
        she would've seen the muscles of Heracles
            the wings of Icarus
            the hunch in your spine
            the bolts in your neck
Had she bothered to listen to the echoes of your soul
        she would've been moved by the sirens' song &
            the Call of the Wild
        she would've heard the cry of the albatross
            the bells of Notre Dame
            the roar of Aslan

Had she traversed the labyrinth of your heart
        she would've found the beast in the center
            could've loved him enough to turn him human
Had she taken off the shackles of her parentage
                the hatred-colored glasses they gave her
        she would've been free to see the spirit of King Hamlet
                      the spirit of Jacob Marley
                      the spirit of us all
We *are* the new Homer
        Chaucer
    the new Dickenses & Dickensons
    the new Bards upon Avon calling the hearts & loins of everyone
We are the classics her great-grandchildren will be reading in school
            great-grandchildren she will not share with you
    because she sought someone at her level
    because she thought you were below her
    because she never knew
        you are so
            far
                above.

Freaky

Excuse me.

Can I get a little

        freaky?

Would you mind?

'Cuz I was just wondering

    how your toes would taste with a touch of honey

        or if it's at all possible to make your sweetness any sweeter

            by pouring on some chocolate syrup

                    heated

Can I do that?

Would that be alright?

And do I use red wine or white?

Which is proper for sipping from supple breasts

    and licking off your inner thigh?

            My, my, my

Or is it better to get drunk off the juice I drink from your cup?

I mean, forget the Tootsie Roll Pop,

    how many licks does it take to get your center creamy?

I don't know, but I'd like to find out

Are you down?

Can I go down

    and up

        and down again

            as you watch?

Or would you prefer a blindfold, as I carry out this execution,
    killing you with every kiss
        as I kiss   everywhere
        and lick   everywhere
        and gently bite,
            if that's alright?
And can I keep going all night?
Would you mind if I
    enter from behind
        and try to find
            that button
            that spot that gets you hot
                with hot hands reachin' 'round
            'til ecstasy's found
Ooo, if I could hear every sound you make
    it would be music to my ears
        and every face would be that of the Goddess
And I'd be delighted to tickle your pink
        your person
with a feather
    a finger
    or a whole hand feeling the smoothness of your skin
        as you feel the smooth silk scarf binding you to the bed
    or you can tie me up instead

I don't care

Do what you dare

    just so long as I get you

        there

            to the point of pure pleasure 'til you peak,

                pouring your passion into my palm

                  finger lickin' good

So what do you say?

Is it okay

    for me to get a little

        freaky?

Alright, you stay right there.

I'll be right back with the ice cream.

Katchupa [for Quintin & Renegade]

My grandmother was the shepherd
        leading her lambs to their cultural slaughter
                through a lack of leading them to their culture
Insistent that her children be born American
                      raised American
                known as American
        she turned her back on the homeland of Cape Verde
                except for the occasional curse word
                and the food
Perhaps this is why I love the taste of a good katchupa
I have not the knowledge of crioulo words or grammar
My college taught me what little I know of my history & culture
I guess it just feels good
        having something of the homeland
                roll off my tongue
                sit in my gut
                      and warm my heart.

Decent Exposure

I wanna be **NAKED!**

I said I wanna get buck **NAKED!**

Right here! Right now!

I wanna rip off every last stitch of clothing

    strip down to nothing

        'til I'm totally bare

            completely exposed

                and just stand here shouting,

    "Here I am, World! Look at me!"

I wanna wave my winkie like a magic wand

    making my minions marvel or dismay at the magic I make.

No!

Better still, I'll use my dick like a detector

Bip bip   bip bip bip bipbipbipbibibibeeeeep!

    and hunt down that really big dick,

        y'know, the guy who first called it … "indecent exposure,"

        and cause him serious pain.

I wanna bring him to his knees

    beat him senseless

    slap him silly

        not … necessarily … with my hands …

            what, with him on his knees and all …

I wanna run free through a field of tall grass
    feeling the blades and soft breezes tickle my body
    running 'til I run out of breath
        out of strength
    spinning 'til I'm dizzy
        then collapse & roll around on the soft, cool ground
            watching stars spin in the kaleidoscope sky
                making time stand still.

I wanna streak through the naked city
    just as naked as it is
        with nothing on … but a good pair of running shoes
        wind whipping over my body
        winkie whipping to and fro
        shocking the onlookers as I pass
        screaming 'til I'm hoarse,
    "Here I am, World! Look at Me!"

I wanna go for a moonlight swim in the warm ocean waters,
    skinny-dipping, while she watches from her night sky throne

Or bathe in the rays of the glorious sun,
    lying naked in the sand in broad daylight
        exposed to the elements and to everyone around

I wanna walk naked in the warm rain,
    feeling the soft summer shower caress my skin

I wanna *get* naked
    and *be* naked
        forever …
            but …

Someone *did* call it ... "indecent exposure"
    and someone *believed* it
        a *lot* of someones believed it
            until almost *everyone* believed it
                so I can't
I wanna do it, but I can't ...
    well, I *could*, but I'd get arrested,
        so I won't
            but I think I've found the next best thing
As I stand before you
    and, instead of baring my skin,
        I bare my soul
    instead of tearing off my clothes and exposing my naked flesh,
        I tear off the façade of my everyday self and
            expose the real me
instead of showing you my winkie,
    I show you my heart
instead of stripping down to nothing,
    I strip down to *something*
        a little bit
            with every poem I read.
It's not nudity, but realer, rawer, nakedness.
I *know* it's the next best thing;
    in some ways, it's even better,
So ... here I am, World.
Look at me.

Watch/er

She enters

Slinking slipping sliding gliiiiiiding in to the room

    sensually, sexually, without meaning to be

                                          and I watch.

She lets her purse fall onto the bureau,

    turns on her stereo   softly, and

        like clockwork, slowly saunters over to the mirror

                                          as I watch.

And I wonder

    I wonder if she knows just how sexy she is

        without meaning to be

            only meaning to be herself

                                          as I watch.

Slowly

Slowly she slides long slender fingers to the back of her head

    releasing from the prison of a bun

        the long thick curtain of night sky

                                          as I watch.

Slowly her neck

    her elegant slender neck, formerly exposed, becomes covered,

        as the curtain falls   past her shoulders

                        down her back

                                          as I watch.

And I wonder if she's honestly doing things slowly   to taunt me

        or if it's just a trick my mind plays on me

                to taunt me

Her hands go through each button on her blouse
    one   by one
        letting the shirt slide like water off her back
            fall like a feather   to the floor.
Not satisfied with this small meal,
    the predator hands attack the button fly of her jeans
               as I watch.
Sitting on the bed, she peels off the second skin of her fruit-bearing thighs,
    then stands and moves to the mirror again
And I wonder why she goes to the mirror every time
    why she needs to watch
      like I need to watch
As the claws of her hands
    release the claws of her bra
    release her perfect breasts from their slavery sling
      which she just lets drop,
        lifeless and empty, to the floor
          and I know how it feels
              as I watch.
She hooks her thumbs around the edges of her panties and
    bending down, she pulls down
She doesn't pull down halfway and wiggle, she doesn't cheat
Rather, she loves the feel of the stretch in her muscles as she pulls
          all the way down
    loves the feel of her hands on her now naked skin
      as she caresses herself all the way back up
        stopping for a moment at those
          oh-so-perfect breasts

        taking a little more time

                here

                        as I watch.

And I watch her look in the mirror at her beautiful form
And I wonder   what she wonders
    if she admires herself like I admire her
        or as much
    or if she somehow finds a tiny flaw or two
        and magnifies them
Finally she floats back to the bed
    and I watch her gently lift her hand,
        to turn off the light, and I can't watch anymore
I lower my hands away from my face, only for a moment
    to activate the night-vision feature on the binoculars they hold.
Then, I can watch
    as she slides under the covers,
        rolls to one side,
            sighs
        and slips away
           slowly
        to sleep.

Here

Here is the key to my closet
    left ajar long ago
        bones spilling out all over themselves
            rushing the dance floor
Here are the demons
    birthed of my head
    howling newborn screams
    being ignored for too long
    now cradled
        cooed
        cared for
    learning to fly away
Here are the torn pages from my journal
    removed from the sealed envelope
    removed from under my pillowcase
    removed from the trash that is never thrown away
    taped together like the puzzle my life is
        only solved
Here is my cat
    meowing to be pet
    purring at newly positive attention
    bag not just untied but torn open
        not to be used again
Here is my shield, sword & armor
    retired from battle now
    rusting stiff & unusable

Here are my clothes

    first gloves, scarves, hat

    then winter coat, light jacket underneath

    then thick, protective boots & three pair of socks

    then sweatshirt, sweater, button-down & two Ts

    next jeans over sweatpants over pajamas over long johns

    lastly boxer-briefs with cartoon print

Here are my clothes

Hold them here as I walk in the cold November rain

    as I stroll the Sahara in its summer

    as I skip through the bad parts of town

        broken glass, stray needles & all

    as I freeze & bake & bleed

    as I come back for more

        but not for my clothes

See, I looked in the mirror the other day

    & my reflection was there

    & the glass didn't crack

    & neither did I

I looked in the mirror the other day

    & I liked what I saw

        so here are my clothes

        hold them here

I don't need them anymore.

Slammed

What's the matter?
Was I not good?
    not good enough for you?
Did I not give it my very best
    not my soul invest
    stab dead center chest
      and let blood
          sweat
            tears spring eternal onto page
              a paper towel soaking up the mess of my life?
Did I not strip down to nothing
    strip down to something enough for you
      expose my heart
        my soul
        myself to you
            naked, save the transparent shield of words
Or were you disappointed with the dance?
    over too quickly
        not enough tease in my strip, I suppose
I used my hands to hold my heart for all the world to view
You wanted them to rip yours out and crush it under shoe
But my pain was not apparent
    my rage not outrageous enough for you
I stayed true to myself
    but managed to screw myself,
      so what was it?

Did I not do enough screaming?

Was my demeanor not demeaning?

           too demeaning?

      Did you miss my meaning?

          or was I not mean

                not obscene

                    too squeaky clean for your far-from-virgin ears

                        longing for me to thrust insert dick *here*

Did I not say "fuck" enough?

Did I not fuck enough?

Did I not get fucked enough?

Well, y'all sho'nuff took care of that, didn't cha?

Message for the Millennium

It's the 21st century & I'm reliving the headlines of my college days
There's a dick with no balls that goes by the name of Bush
He sits in the captain's chair
      playin' massah in the Whitey House
He sends men overseas to play overseers
      whipping other cultures who don't follow his rules
      taking over another slave owner's land for the sake of
            what?
Oil? Money? Vendetta? Protection? Justice? Freedom?
All of the above?
Sitting at the right hand of a man playing God
      is a man in desperate need of a brain … no
          that was '93
This man needs a good, working heart, but still
      between the three of them
          you wonder where Dorothy & Toto are
It's the 21st century & I'm reliving the headlines of days before I was born
Hundreds upon hundreds are dead
      – some bodies never accounted for –
          in the worst attack ever on American soil
      & rumors are spreading
      & people are wondering
          just how much our leaders knew beforehand
              but wondering didn't come fast enough
                  to stop another war
      & today people protest a war no one really understands
          just like with another Dick in the massah's house

But it's the 21st century & it's time to write new headlines
It's time for the uprising against the system
    time for the revolution we pledged so long ago
    time to see a Black
        a Hispanic
        an Asian
        a woman as President
    time to see teachers making an athlete's salary
    time to put all the world leaders on the USS Gandhi
        with nothing but bread & fruit juice
            & wait for the world's greatest treaty to be born
It's the 21st century & there are 2000 songs
            & 2000 poems
            & 2000 essays
            & 2000 stories
    recycling the same old message of love 2000 times each
        every year for the past 2000 years
            the same old message falling on deaf ears
It's the 21st century & it's time for that message to finally sink in
                      deep
                    so deep
                I'm talkin' Titanic deep
                glow-in-the-dark fish deep
        deeper than the center
        deeper than God
                I'm talkin' beyond deep

It's the 21st century & we're just scratching the surface
        but can anyone tell that it's the inside surface
                of our collective casket?
So stop the presses & spread the love
Scratch harder & go deeper
Trade in the dicks in office for organs usually found in chests
Listen to your favorite teachers
        your parents
        your children
        your lovers
        your own souls
Listen
        finally
Listen
        to the message of love
Let's give the headlines
        something else to talk about.

Tainted

I wanted to write you the perfect love poem
I wanted my words to paint pictures of my love in minds, like
    a painter creating a master work of art
        using colors vibrant & vivid & alive with my love
but the colors must've run together to make a sick, dull brown
    or else every color seems tainted with gray
        dull and lifeless, like
the music in my heart,
    song composed on an out-of-tune piano
        creating a melody bittersweet and off-key
    tainting & distorting my harmony
        music falling flat, like
my efforts at the perfect romantic meal
    a breakfast in bed, tainted by sour milk & rotten eggs
        no seasoning in the cupboard
            making things bland & poisoned, like
Chernobyl farmland
    beautiful & bountiful
        life-giving soil now dead
    tainted by waste
        destroyed by human touch & technology, like
the South American rainforests
    dense and populous
        full of life
        of color
        of possibilities
            slashed & burned to oblivion

                    cut down

                    cut short

                    killed, like

my dreams of forever with you

my waterfall of warm memories turned cold

                freezing cold

                freezing my heart

        encased in winter memories

            waiting for spring thaw

                to wash tainted, polluted waters away

I wanted to write you the perfect love poem

I wanted to give you the perfect love

    but my love has been tainted by my broken heart

        poison spilling like mercury from a thermometer

            words of love leaving a sour taste in my mouth

I wanted to write you the perfect love poem

    but I'm old enough to know by now

        that nothing is perfect.

Weight

Can't keep my eyes from the circling skies
Tongue-tied and twisted, just an earthbound misfit, I ...
feel ...
heavy ...
      with the weight of the world on *my* shoulders now
          giving Atlas the rest I've heard him cry for
              Superman the vacay from cape and chafing tights
                  the opportunity to fly *from* trouble
                  the time to remember that Clark Kent
              was once more than just a secret identity
I remember, as a kid, wanting to be the Man of Steel
      tightly tying towel 'round my neck
      feeling cape flap in the breeze I create by running
                      from real life
      needing to escape, even at such a young age
Yes, I know my feet touch the ground
      but only literally
In my mind, I soar above skyscrapers, screaming
      "Look, I can fly!"
Never knew saving the world
      would be such a trying task
Now, cape is noose-like around neck
Now, I ... feel ... heavy ... with the weight of the world on *my* shoulders
      and someone piled on the rest of the universe
          when I wasn't looking

I feel heavy with the weight pushing

                pressing

            oppressing

        but I press on

            push on

                push out roadblocks large as pyramid blocks

                pound on prison walls I made myself

        I am pinned by my responsibilities

              tacked into my wings

                      like butterfly in glass case

                      losing breath

                      deprived of oxygen

Cruel punishment, for see-through wall lets me see the sky

I remember how it was to slip free of slumber

              crawl from cocoon

              spread wings for the first time

    "Look, I can fly!"

Are mental wings forever damaged from the world's touch?

Closed eyes in charter planes

Focus forward over bridges

Watching *others* ride roller coasters

Hell, I can't even climb ladders without shaking

                    quaking

                    causing the fall

                  that's causing this fear

But at night, I still dream of fears forever forsaken
                      Shaken
    not needing wings to climb into night sky
            make love to mistress moon
        'til brother sun shines on me in all *my* glory
            showing me off to oppressive world
            mocking it in its efforts to keep me down
    "Look, I can fly!"
I wake to the weight of the world on *my* shoulders now
    and I am **tired**
        of **feeling**
            heavy!
        want to discharge this debt to its previous owners
            but it seems Atlas went underground
                Superman flew far away
They're probably together at some Dublin pub
    laughing over pints of Guinness at their hapless volunteer
We'll see who laughs last when I
    let go of this world
    let it free
    let it fall
    let it fly out of control
    let it go
Like my predecessor, I try to climb to the nearest, highest mountain
    but the best I can find nearby is a bridge
        Mt. Hope
            how ironic

Hand over shaky hand, I forget fears
    eager to reach my goal, for
        every rung brings me closer to
            disrobing
            dispelling
            disregarding this rock
                this mortal coil
At the top, I kiss the sky
    strip free of bonds and binding clothes
    spread wings like I remember
    and let go
Feeling wind rushing at my body rushing at water below
    but *I don't care*
      I don't see
      I face forward toward horizon
        as mistress kisses sun and me goodnight
      I soar above everything in sight
        and for the first time in forever,
            I …
            feel …
            light …
Look.
I can fly.

Male Nursing

I am a man, like my father before me …
    actually, my father never "grew up" to become a "real" man,
        but that's another poem altogether
I am not woman
    so you will not hear me roar in the pains of labor
I have not uterus with which to shelter life growing
Alas, the greenhouse for budding humanity rests solely
    in the belly of woman
        which I am not
I can never know the euphoria of another growing inside me
                with me
        totally dependent on me
I will never need to cut my cord from someone
    letting her or him breathe on his own
        feed on his own
        bleed on his own
I cannot produce in my bosom
    necessary nourishment for my child
    vital nutrients for his survival
        for which to hold him close to my heart
        look into his eyes
        tell him without words
        how he is my whole world
Yet, in a way
    I can
    I will
    I must

I must let him & his mother know that they can totally depend on me
    must encourage my child to do things for himself
        let him bleed, when necessary
    must provide in my bosom the vital nutrients for his emotional survival
    must take the time to hold him close to my heart
            look into his eyes
            tell him how he is
                      my
                              whole
                                    world

Maybe these words will be enough.

It All Started When... [A Writing Exercise]

It all started when Cain killed Abel

It all started when one person thought there wasn't enough room

    for everyone in the world

        when the world was as large as now

            & the population was just barely in double digits

It all started when the Tower of Babel fell

It all started when the peoples were separated

        languages encrypted

        distances enlarged

        seeds of misunderstanding sowed

It all started when Kronos ate the Gods

    jealous & distrustful of his own children

        the last who sat heavy as a stone

It all started when that deception was complete

        the stone revealed

        the father castrated & banished

        the dictator in the heavens replaced

        by just another dictator

It all started when Paris turned to Helen

    mooning over

    wooing

    winning someone else's prize

It all started when bitter rivalry turned into competition & bribery

        first-sight love turned into infidelity

        cuckoldry turned into war

It all started when Jesus died

It all started when preaching love was seen as an insult
        as a spectacle
        as a threat
It all started when prophet became God
      became martyr
      became myth to end all myths
It all started when legend & prophecy became fact
     & ancient spirituality became fiction
It all started when Caesar ruled the known world
    when Napoleon ruled the known world
    when Charlemagne ruled the known world
    when we discovered that what was "the known world"
     depended on who you talked to
It all started when the explorers explored
    when Columbus discovered
     what others had already claimed for centuries
    when conquering the less advanced
     became an act of heroism
    when stealing & butchering
     became acts of patriotism & nobility
It all started when pigments became barriers & excuses
   for inhumane conditions, treatment & views
It all started when a king denied his people & took their money
     when "the shot heard 'round the world" first rang
      for what was supposed to be freedom
       that never completely came
     when the rest of the world hear the shot
      & fired back at their oppressors

        & when Nietzsche warned far too late

              of the monsters we would become at times like these

It all started when an oedipal complex

        became the fuel of a nation's fire

            when innocents became the scapegoats

    of a twisted man's army

            when cultures were assassinated

    for no other reason than that they could be

            when millions shook in fear of one word:

                            Fuhrer

        & it starts again every day

It starts with the death of every new prophet of love, peace & freedom

        King

        Lennon

        Bhutto

        The next one yet to be named

It starts with every unanswered cry for help

            every frozen homeless person

            every malnourished child

            every prisoner unjustly accused

            every suicide

It starts with every gun shot

            every one-too-many shots of Jack before driving

            every shot of the needle giving imitation joy

                      instant gratification

                      eventual death

It starts with every time someone ignores words like
    No
        Please
            Help
    Stop
            Help
    Need
        Love
            Help

It starts when owning the green paper hammer becomes more important
    than using it to build something better

It starts when false information
    is used as justification
        for conquering & converting another nation

It all started at the beginning of Time

It all started at the beginning of Man

It all starts again
    every single minute
    of every single day

When

When will it all end?

Haiku Hell

I never before
Could write a haiku poem;
Now, they just won't stop!

        I've never written
        So much haiku poetry
        In so little time

                Now, my greatest fear
                Is that I won't stop talking
                In haiku pattern

        Now, wait a minute.
        Even my last three statements
        Were all a haiku

You see what I mean?
This haiku inspiration
Just won't stop flowing

        I can't control it
        And I can't get rid of it
        I can't shut it off

                It just keeps going
                Like that battery bunny
                Drumming through my mind

        Alright! I give in!
        I've no choice but surrender
        I wave my white flag

Come and possess me,
All ye spirits of haiku
Take my heart and soul

In exchange, I ask
That I make only beauty
With your haiku verse

Words flowing freely
Fall into haiku pattern
Give the spirits rise

Days Go By

A self-proclaimed queen pessimist tells me it's sad
    that I cross out the days on my calendar as they pass
I disagree
I say it's respectful
Yesterday is dead
    I need to bury it
        else I would be the carrion feasting on its remains
I say it's cautious
    even responsible
        to fill in gaping holes & prevent myself from falling in
        to block the outlets that shock until they kill
        to close off exits from reality that open only one way
I say it's good health
    to not twist & strain my neck & body
    to rather face forward & see where I'm going
I say it's important & mature
    to focus on a goal
    to plan ahead, not fall behind
Y'see,
Days go by like buses when you're not waiting at the right stop
    & the stop at yesterday is always closed
It's important to publish that information
    so everyone knows
Days go by like deadbeat dads giving birth to ideas
    but only long enough to give them names
        not enough to give them what they need to grow up right

Days go by & they don't come back

Marking the occasion is realistic

It's facing facts

All we really have is today

All we can plan for is tomorrow

    & I refuse to get lost in yesterday anymore

I can't help but see that

    as positive.

Brother

Brother, I need you
> need you to guide me back to that mountain we almost climbed
> need you to help me find it
>> help me find myself
>> help me up
>>> take my trembling hand from the ground it clutches
>> and take me with you to the top this time

Brother, I miss you
> miss your face
>> your voice
>> your presence
>> your essence is missing
>>> here

I miss a piece of me
> miss days I could always count on it being
>>> here
>> days I didn't have to worry about it missing
>> days I didn't have to worry about anything
>>>> missing
>>> about me
>>>> missing
>>>>> you

Brother, I hate you
> hate you for leaving me
>> leaving me only halfway up the mountain
>> while you reached the top
>> leaving me stuck in this town
>> while you chased *our* dreams

      attained *our* goals

    leaving me stranded on this planet

     while you touched the stars

  I hate you for leaving

    leaping

    jumping

    flying

    soaring into the sun

     when my legs feel too weak to even stand

Can you help me stand?

Where are you to help me stand, my brother?

    help me stand, from 3,000 miles away

    help me stand

      and show me the way to the top of that mountain

      show me the way home

      show me the way to reach you

        to hold you

        to tell you

Brother, I love you

  I still love you.

Jay Walker Day

Every October, we celebrate the existence
    of a man who went to other countries
        because he couldn't get funding from his own
We celebrate the day he got lost going the long way around the planet
    celebrate the day he crashed onto someone else's land
        & claimed it for the country he represented
    celebrate the desecration
        degradation
        disassembly &
    near destruction
    of western-hemisphere nations
      & eastern-hemisphere tribes
        as his people built kingdoms on the blood of one
            and the backs of another
We celebrate the day great & diverse nations
    were lumped into one group
        misnamed for the place he *thought* he was going
    celebrate the day they started lumping *other* great nations
        into boats not big enough for *half* their number
    celebrate the dark & twisted legacy of a man
        who spent his last days in a debtor's prison
We hang on to myths that he was the first one here
    just so we can have one more day off from work
        one more day off from our *own* slavery
That's why, every October
    I say, "Fuck Columbus! My birthday's a *three-day weekend!*"
Happy Jay Walker Day, everybody!

True Colors

"I was 700 feet tall once."
    That's how you started
        and I believed you.
Little petite five-foot-something
    tell me you stood taller than some city skyscrapers
        and I believed you
I watched you on stage and looked into eyes like skies
            like ice crystallized
            like Great Lakes
              great big and blue
    purity only slightly tainted by society
        but still beautiful
I hung
    on
        every
            word uttered from those lips
    and I believed it like it was Gospel
        like the Goddess spoke through you
            was you
    paying homage with undivided attention
I wanted to turn back time and hear it all again
    turn back time to the days long ago
        when the radio still had its All Request Saturday Night
            and send you the dedication you said you wanted
                waited for
    but never got

I see your true colors shining through

                        your poetry

      colors both fun and focused

           playful and thoughtful

           whimsical and philosophical

           tragical and beautiful

      shades I'd only seen before in sunsets

           painted vividly in my mind by your words

I wanna dip my brush in your paint

Now, you can take that any way you want it

    but what I mean is

        what I mean is …

           well, yeah, that, too

                but what I *really* mean is …

I wanna paint with your colors

    paint you for the world to see you

        in your colors

        through my eyes

I wanna use my hands in your paint

    dip deep in your bucket

    see how deep you are

    let your colors slip between my fingers

        slide over my skin

        cover me completely

    really feel you

    really know you

    then take my hands

        and streak your colors across a canvas the size of Colorado

  painting those sunsets

    and sunrises

    and the glorious Goddess moon

      in your Goddess colors

  hanging it on the highest mountain peak

    for even the stars to gaze upon in want and wonder

      or maybe it will hang in your home

Yes, it will hang in your home

  to make you understand your wonderful vision

  to make afraid the boa constrictors

    shirtless men

    and other infidels and non-believers

Yes, it will hang in your home

  a gift for you

    as a thank-you for what you give to us all

Yes, it will hang in your home

  as a reminder that you'll never need a lunatic in your shower

    as long as you keep letting us inside

      to see your true colors.

What I Want

I don't want to want you

                                                    I do

I don't want to hear you when you're not there

                                                    I do

I don't want to see you when I close my eyes

                                                  I do

I don't want to smell you on my clothes

        on my sheets

        on my finger

I don't want your essence to linger

I don't want to taste your lips

        or taste your lips

    sweet poison lingering on

I don't want to taste you long after you've gone

                                                  I do

And I don't want to remember you

        remember the feel of your skin

                on my skin

        remember the look of your face

                the flow of your body

                the sound of your voice

        remember the way we used to be

I don't want to remember you

But I don't want to forget

I don't want to want you

I guess you can't always get what you want …

Or do you?

Contemplation

Death without sacrifice is a paradox
Death without sacrifice is an impossibility
Death **is** sacrifice
Life **is** sacrifice
Death is life is death
To be or not to be
    that is *my* question
        my query
        my paradox plague
            playing in my mind over & over on every fuckin' channel
            like that damned <u>Titanic</u> song
I'm watching my gigantic mind-ship sink deep beneath the surface
    of superficiality
        a little white speck in a sea of blackness
        like the yin-yang circle
        like the life-death cycle
For in my life am I dying inside
    in my death might my memory live on
The black plague rages on
    against the machine of my mind
The death debate cannot deliberate
Each side still pleads its case
The brutality of life
    The finality of death
The pain I feel now in life
    The pain I would cause others in death

How can I go on living?

How would I face death?

And how *would* I face death?

Would I cringe

    cower

    cry?

Would I become a coward

    come up to death's door

    knock &

    run away

        like a child at play

            ding-dong-ditch

        & just switch-up

            change my mind

        "Just kidding."

        just kidding myself

or would it be more cowardly

        to walk through the door when she answered

            seeking solace

                shelter

            & sanctuary from the insanity

                of the outside world

        shaking the skeleton hand of my hostess

                    my half-savior

                        half-enslaver

        savoring the flavor of death dessert

            bittersweet?

Maybe I could embrace death fully
   give her the big ol' hug she seems to need
  taking so many
    yet always traveling alone
    give her my deep soul through a deep soul-kiss
  full on the lips
Maybe it's me who feels alone in a crowd of friends
  or maybe I am my own death
    debating the nature of me
      instead of just being me naturally
Maybe it's me who needs a hug
     a kiss
     a sign of understanding
 & if I am death
   am I also life
     in all its tragic beauty
      of self-contemplation
     & contemplation of tragic beauty?
Maybe I think too goddamn much
Maybe I just need to stop thinking
    start living
    start loving my life
      myself
Maybe I just need to scream at the top of my lungs
  confirming my life in order to cheat death
  calling for the world to bear witness to the wonder of me
  capturing on this paper
    the sound

   the feeling of true freedom
     so as to serve as my own witness
       to my own wonder
        at times of further such contemplation
Maybe I can learn
  how to give myself that hug
    when I need it.

Sometimes...

Sometimes, words just sound pretty.

Sometimes, words just sound cool together.

Sometimes, words just seem to flow well and,

    in flowing, form a pretty pattern of similes and metaphors,

        electrifying alliteration and onomatopoeia,

            painting beautiful pictures in our minds

                with their wonderful words.

Sometimes, words just seem to say the right thing

            in the right way

            at the right time,

    moving us, involving us, enticing us, enthralling us

        with their rhythm & rhyme ...

        but sometimes ...

Sometimes, those pretty words,

    those enticing, enthralling, moving words

        don't make any sense.

Sometimes, it's all just an act,

    all smoke and mirrors

        all glamour and glitz, with nothing behind them,

  no meaning no substance, no sense or sincerity,

Nothing.

Sometimes, words just sound pretty, but sometimes ...

Sometimes, words *just sound* pretty.

Sometimes, those words mean nothing.

Sometimes ...

Now How Much Would You Pay?

I stand in the center of chaos
I stand in the eye of the hurricane
I stand in the rubble & debris of ground zero
        as a piece of the world has collapsed in on itself
I stand at the epicenter of this
                building-quake?
No, it's not an earthquake
        because it hasn't left the earth quaking
                in its collective boots
It has barely sent the city shaking in fear & loathing
        at what we have become
For thousands, life has stopped today
For thousands more, life has been irreversibly changed
Yet no more than a few blocks away
        life goes on, like nothing happened
People still stand on street corners
        hustlin' to get by
                get ahead
                get what they can
                        for themselves
        hockin' everything from glass bowls to lost souls
        selling things as trivial as stocks
                and as crucial as someone's next meal
People still stand for themselves
        Wearin' sandwich boards
        Screamin' "Sale! Sale! Sale!"

Can't they see that, beneath that sandwich board
    they are naked?
Can't they hear that the words they scream are really
    "I have a price!"
    "I can be bought!"
    "I can be numbed to the world's pain
        if you pay me enough!"
I just want to take them
    wake them
        shake them from their drug-like
            dollar-induced
            TV-tranquilized
    state of sedation
I want to scream, "Wake up!
    go home to your wives
        your lives
        yourselves
            find the nearest parentspousesiblingchildfriend you can
        hold them close to you
            look into their eyes
                & tell them how you feel
If you can't get to them in person, use a phone
Call collect, if you have to
Who cares if you "save 'em a buck or two"
        "dial down the center"
    or "just dial zero"?

What kind of deal do you want?

What kind of price would you pay

    to be able to say "I love you"

        and hear it said back

    to be able to "reach out & touch someone"

        feel that someone touch back

      while you're both still able to feel it?

Does it depend on how much a life's worth?

        how much a thousand lives cost?

How many people have to die

How many others have to cry

    before we finally learn to see eye to eye?

I beg you all to stop

      look

      listen to all around you

    before we cross this road again

I beg you all to see the real enemy

We are not under attack by some foreign state

    for there are no foreigners, save the ones we make

We are not at war with anyone but ourselves

    & our own hate

    our own fear

    our own minds

So, Uncle Sam, call your planes

        tanks &

        troops

          home

My comrades in red, disarm your nuclear missiles
Brother sheik, kill your germ warfare
A guy on TV just told me there's a sale on Lysol
      but I'd pay anything so that Mr. Clean *and* Brawny
          could together be strong enough
              to clean up this mess
I'd pay any price to the store that can sell me
      an industrial-sized, maximum-strength dose
          of compassion
              camaraderie
              community on the global scale
What about you?
I'm talkin' to you, America! What about you?
You just kept laughin' as we sang
      "What's so funny 'bout peace, love & understanding?"
Well, are you still laughing, America?
What about you, America?
What price would you pay for a little piece?
Will it take another life
      another thousand lives
      another million lives?
When will this layaway on love finally be paid?
When can unity finally leave the store & be brought home?
When, America?
I'm talkin' to you
I'm reachin' out to you
      to all America
      to all the world!

I'm comin' to you with the answers in my hands
                the cure in my heart
    comin' to you with my arms outstretched
        offering a big, long, healing hug
I'm comin' to you with a chance at world peace
      so that not one more innocent life is lost
It's the deal of the century!
Now how much would you pay?

Random Haiku, Senryu & Tanka

How can someone slam
With just a simple haiku?
Tonight we find out

        New England weather
        Makes for much complaining and
        For great poetry

                I would much prefer
                To walk around in the nude
                But I don't like jail

        My soul is dying
        Capital punishment for
        Killing off my dreams

Hot and humid days
Sweating people ask of me,
"How can you wear jeans?"

        Countless flowers bloom
        From the breath of poets
        Beauty ears can see

                Humorous haiku
                Comic relief for the night
                A poet at play

        In cemeteries,
        A waste of fertilizer
        Cows don't eat the grass

"Gezundheit," I said,
As he spoke of his haiku.
He was not amused

Sweet summer showers
Do for my soul what they do
For streets and flowers

My soul is in need
Of a thimble to protect
From life's little pricks

Isn't it scary
How normal conversation
Can become haiku?

Leda and the Swan
Painted so beautifully
But wasn't she raped?

It's all fun and games
'til someone loses an eye
Then, it's keep-away!

I see the beauty
Lyrical motion of all
Life is a poem

My full, legal name
Is Jason Eric Walker;
I don't care who knows.

I am Narcissus
Drowning in my own ego
But who cries for me?

Poet with no shame
I have two chapbooks for sale
Five dollars apiece!

                                    The coming of spring
                                Gives almost ev'rything life
                                        I am dead inside

                    Her eyes are the skies
                  That cloud for beautiful words
                      Sweet April showers

I am in the mood
To write another haiku
But if I should add
Two seven-syllable lines
Haiku then becomes tanka

                    Black mistress reaching
                   Seduction into darkness
                    Sweet embrace of death

                                        Hey, you behind me!
                                    If you're gonna ride my ass,
                                         Put on a condom!

                    Watching you, I know
                  You are the greatest poem
                       I will ever write

Paying for Past Crimes

I am the second gunman on the grassy knoll
    assassin anonymous for eternity
Too old or
    possibly
        too dead to reveal my identity
        or other secrets
I am Hitler! Sieg Hiel!
    megalomaniacal mass murderer
        moving man's emotions
            with words of hatred in the guise of national pride
Waging war on the world
    almost winning
        then whining & whimpering
            (which is how this all started, anyway)
Closing my own curtain like the coward I was
    killing myself at the end
        proving quitters never win
I am the Southern plantation owner
    building a legacy for my blood
        with the blood
        on the backs of the oppressed
I am the oppressor overseer
    whip in hand whirling wailing
        as I'm watching wincing and whining
        as I work the will from the backs of the Blacks

I am Caesar

    Emperor

    Explorer

    Executioner

I came, I saw, I conquered countries countless

    and killing those who stood in my way

        assimilation to the point of almost annihilation

            ancient Borg before Roddenberry days

Betrayed by best bud Brutus

    for being too ambitious

        what a bitch

I am Pilate, Caesar's servant

    sentencing savior to be slain

        then trying to wash my hands of it all

            can you say OCD?

I am Cain

    my brother's keeper turned killer

        damned forever for my fury

            unforgiven for forsaking fellow flesh

I am evil incarnate

    captured now in this carcass

        condemned for all eternity

            to pay the price for my past crimes

I have been all these things

    or at least one

        I must have been

            it's my only explanation

            my only salvation

I must have done something horrible in a past life
to deserve this one

Anakin's Lament

I can't explain it
    but long ago, I discovered
        that I can move things with my mind
I found that, if I reach out with my feelings
    I can see you all for what you truly are
        then, I can reach you
            lift you
                move you so that you feel moved
It is an awesome responsibility to put in the hands of one so young
    but fate is not without a sense of irony
        placing me in the hands of slave masters
                people who won't hear me
        telling them they are slaves themselves
                people who stop me
        from being free, even when it means
            also freeing themselves
Every time I think someone has freed me
    I find that I've merely been passed to another owner
                & another owner
                & another owner
                & **damn it!**
        I just want to be free!
The constant moving has me dizzy
The beatings from the overseer called life have left me sore

The prison of my existence has made me cagey
    & I am angry at the world for its hand in this
        spinning out of control, as it does
            falling farther & faster into chaos when I
want

order!

Order in this court!

The Honorable Jason E. Walker presiding
    because the only things I have left are shreds of honor
        which is still more than I can say for you
            sitting in your big houses
                your thrones
                    your benches, judging me

Well, you are removed from office

Now, *I* am your judge
    your jury
    your executioner, if need be

You are charged with the crimes of judging me
        holding me back
        holding me down
        hurting me with your words
        kicking me while I'm down
        & enjoying it

Now, I find you guilty
    & the punishment is death

I raise my hands
        weapon ablaze bright burning rage red
                glowing crimson with all the hate within me
                        & before I bring this down upon your heads
        I offer only these words:
                "May God have mercy on your souls,
                      because *you* never gave *me* any
                          to offer you now."

Magnetic

There is a place where tragic beauty grows
        on the walls of your refrigerator
Fitting that your feelings are put where they can be kept
                                                  cold
I am drawn to your magnets
        the way I am forced to witness the 100-car pile-up
                that our relationship has become
I want to place my heart next to yours on these walls
        remember what it is to be close to you
                but we are oddly polarized
                      opposite enough to attract
                      Alike enough to repel
                            So that we hover, almost touching
                                Almost
                                          But not quite
                              Leaving each other hanging in limbo
I want to place my heart next to yours on these walls
        But it is too heavy with scar tissue from past damage
My mind traces along the edge of this one here
        Left by she who forced me where I didn't belong
                            Didn't want to be
        She who left me there just when I started to like it
I read that you have given up
        Right when I started to believe
                That our love can get us through this

Now I know why this scar throbs right now
I feel my heart crack along this line
   Hear the deafening shatter &
   See the shards scatter
I look for the pieces
        Among the magnetized rubber words on your refrigerator
           So that I can place my heart next to yours on its walls
        But there will never be enough blank tiles
           To spell out all the things I want to say.

Remembering to Breathe

Last night, we lost power
When I say, "we lost power,"
    I don't mean "we" my house
      Don't mean "we my street
    I mean the whole block lost power,
        As I watched from my porch.
While others lit candles
      Searched for flashlights
      Cursed the darkness
I saw the light
      As I watched from my porch
I saw the light from the sky
Faint pinpricks in the cardboard lid of midnight blue
    Grew bright as diamonds
        And I saw stars shine … in the city!
With the moon running my follow spot
    I performed a soliloquy of silence
        Speaking volumes in homage of night and brilliance
It reminds me of that weekend in Maine
    The sun as my alarm clock,
    Washing naked in a stream,
    climbing mountains figurative & literal,
    dinner from campfire,
    moon for a nightlight
    crickets' lullaby, &
        so many stars bespeckled the sky
        so many stars overtook the sky

    so many stars pinpricked holes in the sky …
     and I could breathe again
I've never felt so free
  and with the blackout,
    I saw glimpses of brilliance in the blackness of memory.
Did you ever notice that the brighter the lights get down here,
  the less you truly see of the heavens?
And you can't hear the moon share her secrets past the traffic
        past the hustle & bustle
        past the bump & grind
        past the goddamn **noise!**

My life is like city nights
  with city lights
    the city fights against nature's way
Incandescence
Phosphorescence
Neon essence shining brighter than stars
    blinding me from my view of dreams
      from my vision of heavens above
      from true power
       true beauty
       true light
Swimming upstream against the mainstream
Swept away by the current of constant conformity
Drowning in the mundane drizzle
     drivel dribbling down the screen
      of my idiot box of life

City screaming white noise so loud, I'm deaf
                               dumb
                               numb from monotony
         of materialism mandated by society
              making manacles for me
              chaining me to my responsibility
I am trapped in the portable prison of this existence
            masquerading as a life
            parading in plain sight
                 like everything's alright
Take off the mask & see my strife
                 my strength draining
      from lack of oxygen
              gagging on values force-fed
              choking on the stale stench of status quo
              strangling the life out of my dreams with its bare hands
              holding me down with the weight of
                    the need to make a living
                         make a buck
                            get the **fuck** out of here!
I can't be making a living,
      'cause I'm not making it
           And this ain't living.
Society has put me in a box,
      possibly preparing me for the inevitable
               for the eventual
      but not now
         not now

I'm not dead yet!
I'm not,
    but I'm dying inside
        and I need to remind myself that I'm still alive
            need to break free from this box
            need to **get the fuck out of here!**
                rip off my clothes
                run back to Maine
                revel in newfound freedom
I need to baptize myself in that stream again, and
    born again, I will climb that mountain again
When I get to the top,
    I will cry freedom to the open sky
        preaching to the choir of birds
        stretching arms out toward the sun
        basking in the glow of nature's glory
        and I will wait
             wait for the moon
                to shine her spotlight on me
                  again
            wait for the stars
                to pinprick diamond-sized air holes
                  in the sky
            wait for my heart
                to sing in homage
                    to night & brilliance
        wait
            to breathe again.

March 20th, 2003

Ladies & gentlemen, congratulate me

I've got cause to celebrate

    'cause today …

Today is my anniversary

    is *the* anniversary of the day I was born again

        the day I was released from prison

            found the true road home

        and started walking

    the anniversary of the rebirth of my innocence

        of the day I remembered how to love myself

        the day I learned what love truly is

Today is the anniversary of the day I fell

Yes, folks, love at first sight does happen

    & I'm living proof

Oh, I've written more love poems than I've got body parts

    but I never really knew anything about it at all

        until I saw

            him

& at first sight, I knew what kind of man I wanted to be

    at first sight, I heard a heart in my chest that I forgot was beating

    at first sight, I was full of something besides myself

        something realer than the tangible

It was like déjà vu

I knew I loved him before I met him

    but I could *not* have dreamed into life a being so

            perfect

His skin so soft & eyes so big & brown
    looking up at me so lovingly
        as I stroke his hair & watch his smile grow
It starts slyly, at the corner of his mouth
    then creeps across his lips
    then widens until it's huge
        & bright
        & beautifully
            toothless

Well, he's got a couple that have come in on his right side
    & I love the way his hair has red highlights
        just like his mother
    & I love the way it's just starting to really curl in the back
        just like his father
    & I love the way he laughs so full & loud
    & I just love the way he says my name:
            "Dada"
My heart leaps & turns & dances like Baryshnikov
My heart sings & rejoices like a Winans brother
My heart screams & cheers like a New England sports fan
    at the turn of the 21st century
My heart beats like
    a newborn baby
    all for him
    all for this *beautiful*
        beautiful

beautiful

beautiful boy

I never thought I'd fall in love with someone of the same gender

I never thought I'd fall in love like this

  never thought love could *be* like this

      but that was all before I held my newborn son in my arms

          one year ago today

So, everyone, congratulate me

    for true love is

        is true cause to celebrate.

Numb to the Gift

God gave me a gift
    wrapped it in my voice box
        cords as ribbons holding things in place
Inside the package
    was dynamite
God gave me a gift of dynamite
    wrapped it in my voice box
    set it above the burning in my heart & soul
    sat back to watch the imminent fireworks
God gave me a gift of dynamite
    set it ablaze
    set it to explode like Roman candles on the 4th of July
    set it to shoot out brimstone beauty
        pyrotechnic pleasure & pain
        truth in all its shades
    against a backdrop of blackish-blue
God gave me a gift of dynamite
    & the tools to light it
        but I lacked the skills
            the training
            the knowledge of how
                when
                where to light it
God gave me a gift of dynamite
    like giving matches to a child

I'm an adult now, or reasonable facsimile therein
      & all these years of playing with fire have left me so badly burned
           that you couldn't count the scars
                without looking under scars
I have no flesh left, only scar tissue
      & I can't tell if the fuel for my fire has finally run out
           or if I've just grown numb to it
      tissue too dense to let the sensation reach my sensors
God gave me a gift of dynamite
      the tools to light the fuse
      & the fuel to keep the fire burning for a long time
Perhaps that fire is still burning
      but I can't feel it.

Your Fox to Her Grapes

You have tasted her fruit & know how sweet her juice can be
    but *she* is owner of her vineyard
        no one else
            including you
This left you like the fox
    calling sour the grapes you once found
        so enticing
Her land, though, is not as ugly & barren
    as you would like others to believe
The view of her coastline is still glorious at sunrise
Her rolling hills still provide an unobstructed view of the sky
    as stars sparkle & the moon rises high
The roots of her vine plunge deep into a rich soil
        drink long on her clear rivers
        give birth still to luscious fruit
    & everyone knows that wine only gets better with time
Also like the fox, your shy nature hides a vicious streak
    released when perceiving attack
        even when it's only imagined
You bear your words like teeth
    tear her psyche like flesh
    rip apart the work she put into this earth of her
In the end, the only thing you succeeded in ruining
    is the seventeen-year-old vine of your friendship with her
        a vine planted by you both
        nurtured by you both
        harvested by you both

       a vine that needs you both
        in order to exist
         to grow
         to blossom
You are too much like the fox
  calling grapes bitter out of your own bitterness
  attacking with vicious bite to your words
  behaving too crazily to be trusted
You have proven yourself unworthy of her fruit
  & are forever banished from her vineyards
    the walls between you growing stronger with distance
Your vine will never grow again
  but others become more bountiful with care & time
    which she used to give to you & the vine you shared
She will drink plentiful of herself
  while you grow thirsty
You are too much like the fox
  but your attacks no longer get through her walls
    so stop
Be once more that fox in the story
You have done your crying of "sour grapes"
Now turn
  & skulk away.

Jukebox

Life puts a jukebox in the minds & hearts of everyone
Punch in a date & listen to what song comes up

<u>I</u>

05-20-2003
Say it loud
       Say it clear
              You can listen as well as you hear
I'm looking for your echo in my infant son's tears
       but I can't hear it
Perhaps he needed to be a newborn *after* your passing
       as the song goes
              or maybe it's that I stopped listening to you so long ago
                      that I forgot what you sound like
Now, I will never remember
I don't know how that makes me feel
You are dead & I don't know how that makes me feel
It's not that I feel nothing
I am not numb from the cold of your absence
You've been gone in every *other* sense of the word
       for some time now
I am not empty without you
I am able to keep more of myself without you there to take
I am not numb
I am not empty

I am not lacking feeling
        or anything else that wasn't there when I had you
Something's here
I just can't put a name to it
        or I can but it feels strange
Naming this feeling is like calling you Dad
The truth of it
        makes it no less
                strange
It is strange to feel this way at your loss
It usually comes in time
        after someone dies
It feels strange not to miss you
It feels strange not to need the five stages
It feels strange to feel instead
                finished
It feels strange to feel closure
        but that's what I feel
Feeling strange doesn't make it any less a sense of closure
        just like feeling estranged doesn't make you any less
            my dad

II

05-21-2003
Sorry, I never told you
        All I wanted to say
I had so much to say to you but I didn't

So many others told me to give you so large a piece of my mind
        I'd be the poster-child for do-it-yourself lobotomies
So many others told me to write you a letter
        that rivaled the country's Declaration of Independence
        that declared the reasons for *my* independence from *you*
So many others told me to send shock waves of negativity
        down that phone wire so hard, you'd be deaf
                but what's the point?
What's the point of making you deaf to words you won't hear, anyway?
What's the point of declaring independence from you
        of telling you I don't want you
                need you in my life
        when you were never really there for me?
What's the point of breaking you off a piece of something
        that you won't digest?
That's what I told myself
        about why I never told you
I thought I was okay with not telling you
        but not having you here to not tell
                leaves me with these words
I don't want these words
I just kept them so that I didn't give them to you
        not to hoard them from you
        not to hide them out of spite
No, keeping these words from you was as much about you
        as the words themselves
                which weren't

I wear them as badges on the inside of my chest
I post them on the bulletin board of my brain
  like a checklist for ensuring emotional safety
I stake it on your lawn like a warning sign
  to remind myself that reaching out to you
    will take my hand off
Beware of Dad
I keep them in my verbal bank account
  because you're not worth the price of spending them
    & if you think that's about you
      then you're not listening
  & I was okay with that
    until you weren't there to not listen
Now, I'm holding onto these words for no one
  so I'm offering these words up now, in this poem
    hoping that you're finally listening somewhere
And I know you're shining down on me from heaven …
  but I don't
    I don't know where you are
    don't know if you're shining
      shivering
      or burning
    if you've been damned
      forgiven
        or recycled like flimsy tin
I like that last thought
 like thinking that you'll get a second chance
   & do it right this time

I like the second thought, too

It makes me think that everyone has a chance

   makes me believe in the righteousness of love

The first thought doesn't please me

       except in that it provides a sense of justice

            knowing that everyone can be held accountable

                      liable

                      responsible

          for wrong-doings & acts not based in love

Still, I'd like to think that you are reaching the Gates now

        that God has my face

           greets you with open arms

           says to you

   what I always wanted you to say to me:

"It's okay, son. I know you tried.

    I'm here now, always have been & always will be,

       so let it out, son.

          It's alright.

              Everything's alright now."

III

05-23-2003

I've been 'fraid of changin' 'cause I built my life around you

            built my excuses around

   your excuses

   your influence

      but you're not here anymore

         & I can either find a new scapegoat

                or face the changes

                      I always needed to make

Now the last of the guests are gone

Now it's just you & me

For the first time ever

For the last time ever

      we are in the same room & you are quiet

Still, without even trying to make the usual spectacle of yourself

      you were the center of attention

I don't envy you, though

Instead, I look at you & can't hold back the tears any longer

I don't miss you

  don't mourn your loss

Like I said, we lost each other a long time ago

      & I finally stopped looking for you

I don't reflect on your early demise

The way you treated yourself

      I'm almost surprised this day didn't come sooner

I'm glad you're not in pain anymore

I just feel sorry for you

I wish you could've known your grandchildren better

  wish you could've known your *children* better

  wish you could've known your*self* better

I look at you in the suit we picked

      & think about how we found it in your apartment

            already laid out, with a belt hanging nearby

You knew this day was coming
    & you still kept playing games with our heads
        with our hearts
        with your own health

Attempts to reach out were just too late
    & you were forced to leave things unresolved for you
        but not for me

I resolved our issues without you there

I feel guilty in that I don't feel guilty

My lack of contact with you wasn't out of spite, bitterness or hatred

It came from a need for self-preservation
    from a feeling of exasperation
        of hopelessness
        of acceptance of the fact that
    you'd never change

You made your casket
    & now you have to lie in it

I made my peace with that awhile ago
    so I cry for you now, not because I miss you
        but because *you* missed *me*
        missed *out*

The other day, I rocked my son to sleep
    & I wondered if *we* ever had moments like that
        when *I* was an infant

I don't want my son to ever doubt

I want him to *know*

   want him to *remember*

   want to be the opposite of your example

      be the example you could never be

Oh, I found elsewhere what I needed from you

       & you *did* give me the perfect example of what *not* to be

         so I didn't miss out *too* much

     but no one else could give you what you wouldn't take

For that, I'm sorry

    But time makes you bolder

       Children get older

         & I'm getting older, too

           I'm getting older, too …

Life puts a jukebox in the minds & hearts of everyone

The dates in late May 2003 are the codes

    for the songs that remind me of you

I am holding my son now

     & wondering what beautiful music will sound

        in the dates to come.

Sifting Through the Ashes of Me

I am searching for phoenix
    in the black ash and soot of stagnation
    in the death of stillness
        rising to life bold majestic
    born anew
I am searching for the freedom in flight and fiery existence
I seek to soar to the sky
    holding tightly to tail feathers
    taking off into the sun
    letting sol consume soul
    growing brighter with a fuel eternal
Let me wear the Ring of Fire like a wedding band
    symbolizing the blessed union of gentle beauty and fierce passion
            of creation and destruction
            of death and life
Bring me to the mouth of the volcano
Stand me in the path of its molten flow
Bathe me in the pool of liquid rock
My skin from within will bubble and pock and fall away
The ashes from me will serve as fertile soil
    give birth to beauty
    to new life
    to myself again
I want to burn with a passion that consumes me
    until there is nothing left but ash
        from which I will rise far more brilliant than the past

For I feel I am in shards
        like something made of glass
                cold, transparent, in pieces
I tried putting me back together with glue
        but it still feels like a piece is missing
I can't hold anything like this
Better to put me back into the fire
        melt me down into shapeless matter and
        let life mold me into something shiny and new
                something beautiful
                something complete
I am searching for phoenix inside myself
I long to hold in my heart that passion all-consuming
        whose flames fueled me in the past
                engulfed me
                incinerated and obliterated
                burning every fiber of my being
                      until there was nothing left but ash
                                        blackness
                                        emptiness
                                        stagnation
                                        death
I feel dead inside
But death, I know, is never final
Just as the sphere of rock is seamless
        so life has no definitive endpoints
That which we call death simply prepares us for a new manner of existence

I know that, if I look hard enough
            long enough
     I will find myself born anew in my remains

These words

These thoughts

These dream images I share

It is simply me
       sifting through the ashes of me
            trying to spark the flames of passion
                  that will give this phoenix rise.

www.ingramcontent.com/pod-product-compliance
Lightning Source LLC
Chambersburg PA
CBHW050206130526
44591CB00035B/2268